SELF-HELP WORKBOOK FOR THE ANXIOUSLY ATTACHED

A Comprehensive Journal To Change Your Attachment and Your Relationship

ROMI SIEGEL

SELF-HELP WORKBOOK FOR THE ANXIOUSLY ATTACHED

A Comprehensive Journal To Change Your Attachment and Your Relationship

Reflective prompts and exercises to help you identify your attachment patterns and shift towards secure best practices.

"TO CREATE A RELATIONSHIP YOU'VE NEVER EXPERIENCED YOU HAVE TO BECOME SOMEONE YOU'VE NEVER BEEN."

You are right! Discovering and healing your anxious attachment is challenging and overwhelming. It is also one of the most fulfilling steps you can take toward a healthy relationship. Welcome to the beginning of your anxious attachment journey. My name is Romi, I am a fellow anxious attacher, certified relationship coach, and NLP practitioner specializing in attachment trauma and its manifestation in adult relationships. I'm here to help you discover how your anxious attachment style translates into your relationship.

Let me start by telling you that you are doing a fantastic job facing your insecurities and working on yourself. I went through my healing journey a few years back, when I ended a meaningful relationship. So I get it and want you to know you are not alone. With the help of this journal, you will learn about the challenging aspects of your attachment style and start to rethink and rewire your automatic trigger reactions.

This journal is designed to follow a path of anxious attachment discovery, through exercises, and journal prompts, and it walks you through the most critical aspects of the healing process. You will learn about your triggers, patterns, and communication styles. You will learn healthy self-soothing, communication, reflecting instead of reacting, and effective problem-solving and conflict de-escalation.

ROMI

CONTENTS

THIS WORKBOOK BELONGS TO

_____

WHAT IS AN ATTACHMENT STYLE?

According to attachment theory, the relationship with our parent figure or primary caregiver is the foundation of all relationship dynamics in adulthood. **Attachment styles are used to identify how we relate to others in our life, form relationships, manage conflict and cope on an interpersonal basis.** Attachment styles happen on a spectrum, so we all exhibit our attachment traits to varying degrees.

Our attachment style develops in early childhood, based on the relationships with our primary caregiver. Children have basic needs to be met, such as; soothing, emotional support, love, care, etc. When we are in tune with our primary caregiver, who can meet our needs, we will likely develop a secure attachment style. If they don't meet our needs, then an insecure attachment forms. There are three types of insecure attachments, anxious-preoccupied, dismissive-avoidant, and fearful-avoidant, also referred to as disorganized.

WHAT IS ANXIOUS ATTACHMENT?

Attachment is how we relate to our partners, based on how we learned to give and receive love when we were children. Anxious, preoccupied, or ambivalent attachment relationships are influenced by a concern that our need for intimacy, love, and affection will not be reciprocated by our significant other. People with an anxious attachment style are concerned with the emotional availability of their partner or others close to them, such as friends or family members.

Anxious attachers need closeness and intimacy but question whether their partners will meet their emotional needs. Autonomy and independence can make them feel insecure. In addition, they can become distressed if they experience inconsistency or a behavioral pattern change from their partner. **Their main concern in a relationship is their fear of rejection and abandonment,** which has a profoundly negative impact on their decision-making and how they relate to conflict and problem-solving in the partnership.

Our anxiously attached relationships are characterized by the impact of low self-esteem and self-worth and the constant concern that others will not reciprocate our love.

We crave intimacy but also remain anxious about whether our partner is able and willing to meet our emotional needs, even when they prove their love for us over and over again. Autonomy and independence in relationships can make us feel anxious. In addition, interpreting our partner's behavior patterns as insincere or inconsistent activates our attachment wound.

Anxious attachment shows up in our relationships in a variety of ways:

➤ Needing constant contact and support from our partner
➤ A constant **need for reassurance** that we are good enough
➤ **Hypersensitivity to rejection and abandonment**
➤ Being overly sensitive to other's actions and moods
➤ **Negative self-view and self-worth**
➤ Difficulty setting boundaries, often infringing on the boundaries of others
➤ The impulse to fix, save, or caretake
➤ Being afraid or incapable of being alone
➤ Ruminating and over-analyzing the small things
➤ Catastrophizing even in the simplest situations
➤ **Placing our partner on a pedestal**, embellishing them with imagined traits
➤ Focusing on people's potential, rather than who they actually are
➤ **Attaching prematurely** to people

WHAT DOES ANXIOUS ATTACHMENT LOOK LIKE IN RELATIONSHIPS?

Anxious attachment appears in our relationships in many forms, but the most prominent sign is a deep fear of abandonment and rejection. This fear produced many coping mechanisms, most of which have become so ingrained in us that we consider them normal personality traits. Here are the most notable ones:

Never saying no. Self-neglect is a survival strategy to keep love in our lives. As anxious attachers, we tend to say 'yes' to things we don't agree with or don't want. If, as children, we didn't get consistent love and attention, then we learned to perform or work for love. This often meant hiding our true selves and needs to please a parent figure and be an easy child. This pattern is carried into our adult relationships, where we struggle to say 'no' due to an internalized fear of rejection. We believe that being agreeable means being lovable, so we people-please, we always say yes, and we volunteer to help, fix, or save.

Not setting boundaries. The lack of boundaries shows up in adult relationships more than we notice. Most of us with anxious attachment don't know how to set or respect healthy boundaries. Have you ever caught yourself not telling your partner that their behavior causes you pain and anxiety? Or perhaps you crossed your partner's boundaries by repeatedly doing something that triggers them. Healthy boundaries are there to protect us. They are the halfway point between how much we can love and respect ourselves and our partners. Setting boundaries isn't selfish or demanding; however, anxiously attached people find it incredibly hard because they grew up having to neglect them to get closer to their parent figure.

Pretending to be okay. Masking our mental state and feelings is another coping mechanism for the anxiously attached. This developed as a response to consistently not having our needs met in early childhood. We learned not to share our needs or ask for what we want. This behavior resurfaces in our adult relationships, where we don't speak our needs and don't want to appear disagreeable. Instead, we follow our partner's plan or way of living, molding ourselves into the person we think they would like. This is highly detrimental to the relationship, as it gives our partner an inauthentic version of us that we must live up to. Eventually, this builds up so much resentment that our unexpressed needs come back in anger outbursts, nagging, or nitpicking.

Assuming instead of asking. One of the most common problems I encounter is that people are afraid to ask their partner to clarify their thoughts or behavior. Instead, they use their imagination to fill in the blanks, making wild assumptions about even the most innocent situation. Catastrophizing is a prevalent anxious trait. Research suggests that when children are subjected to trauma in the long term, they develop an overactive amygdala. The amygdala is the part of our brain responsible for processing emotions. It is activated when we encounter a threat or perceived threat, and it contributes to outsetting our fight, flight, or freeze responses. For those children who were subjected to neglect and abuse and had to learn to fend for themselves in one way or another, this part remained overactive even in their adult years. That is why some may be more inclined to catastrophize in a threatening situation. This can look like noticing our partner acting differently, and instead of asking what the reason for the change is, we make up stories that usually reflect negatively on us.

Developing an over-focus on the partner. A lot of anxious attachers exhibit an over-focus on the partner. As children, if our needs weren't consistently met, we had to learn to 'survive' by adapting to our environment.

In this case, we developed an over-focus on the parent or caregiver. This helped us decide when and how to approach them with our needs. As adults, anxious attachers tend to place an overfocus on their partner in order to get closer and build a connection. This can look like taking care of their needs, giving them extra attention, or going along with all their plans without question. While a healthy interdependent relationship relies on both partners working to meet each other's needs, an anxious attachment relationship can be rather one-sided. The anxious partner often gives beyond their means, with the other partner either not noticing this or simply leaning into the situation comfortably. This can quickly reverse and escalate, building up tension and resentment in the relationship.

Not speaking our needs. As children, we learned to put ourselves second while developing an over-focus on the parent. Consequently, we learned that our needs and wants don't matter and started placing ourselves after everyone else. By default, in our adult relationships, we put our partners first and neglect to speak up for ourselves. This behavior is usually accompanied by a number of insecurities. We fear speaking our needs because we think that stating them or expressing a boundary will make us appear needy or difficult. The truth is that there are no needy people, only people with unmet needs.

Thinking that we are difficult to handle. As anxiously attached, we are unaware of how our unchecked activating strategies can trigger our protest behaviors. This makes us think we are demanding, needy, clingy, argumentative, and irrational. This is often mirrored back to us through our partners, especially if we don't understand that unspoken and unmet needs activate anxiously attached wounds and show up as adult tantrums. When we encounter a threat or perceived threat – usually by thinking that our partner is rejecting or abandoning us – we get activated. This means that we lose control over our thoughts and behavior to the point where we are completely preoccupied with our partner and our relationship until we re-establish contact with our attachment figure (our partner). We cannot think about anything else; we put our partner on a pedestal, idealize our relationship, and believe this is our only chance at love. If the conflict resolves, our nervous system gets regulated, and we return to normal. If not, we try to reestablish the connection with our partner through protest behaviors. These can be anything from excessive phone calls and text messages to picking fights, threatening to leave the relationship, or stonewalling our partner. These behaviors might come across as childish or difficult, but they all reflect an unmet need and a core wound from childhood.

WHAT DOES IT FEEL LIKE TO HAVE AN ANXIOUS ATTACHMENT STYLE?

Often worrying about being rejected or abandoned by our partner	Frequently trying to please and gain the approval of our partner
Feeling threatened, angry, jealous, or worried that our partner no longer wants us when we spend time apart	Using subtle ways of manipulation and gaslighting to stay close to our partner, or to get them to do what we want
Overreacting to things that we see as a threat to the relationship	Wanting closeness and intimacy in a relationship, but worrying about whether we can trust or rely on our partner
Choosing partners who need fixing, saving, or taking care of, or partners who cannot commit	Overly fixating on the relationship to the point where it consumes much of our life
Fearing infidelity and abandonment	Tying our self-worth in with relationships
Constantly needing attention and reassurance from others	Having difficulty setting and respecting boundaries
Placing reassurance and validation outside of us, often expecting them from our partner	Having people-pleasing tendencies to keep our partner in our lives, or prove our worth and value

BECOMING AWARE OF YOUR ANXIOUS ATTACHMENT

A common theme I see with anxiously attached people is that they're either unaware of their attachment style or don't know how it impacts their relationships. Many anxiously attached people have no idea how their attachment style developed. They had loving and caring parents and a perfect childhood. But in reality, our brain has a pesky way of deleting and blocking traumatic experiences, and some information gets completely erased. So how do we start recognizing our anxious attachment?

To begin the healing process, we must first become familiar with our patterns, triggers, and our reactions to them. If they are not apparent, we must find alternative information sources. Try observing your behavior, pause, and pay attention to how you react and behave. Talk to your current or ex-partner about it. Try to witness your family dynamics and your parent's communication styles. Speak to your friends. Perhaps they observed patterns that you did not notice. Try journaling about your past relational experiences. Can you spot recurring themes? Is there an overarching pattern to all of your romantic partnerships? What can you notice? Paying attention to how you choose partners, how you treat people, and how let them treat you will reveal a lot of important information about your relationship patterns.

MISTAKES TO AVOID ON YOUR HEALING JOURNEY

When we first discover our attachment style, it is revealing and overwhelming at the same time. It explains our past behaviors and reactions and directly describes why and how we get triggered. However, we all encounter a few common mistakes as we get absorbed in attachment theory and discover ourselves through the lens of anxious attachment. Let's walk through the most common ones:

Overestimating our problems. Attachment styles happen on a spectrum, meaning that some of us are on the more extreme end, while others have a mild anxious attachment. However, our attachment style is only one part of our multilayered personalities, and they don't mean that there is something fundamentally or unchangeably wrong with us. Securely attached people also experience relationship problems such as misunderstandings, feeling frustrated and unhappy, so relational problems are not only the byproduct of our attachment styles.

Overestimating the problem will only hinder the healing process. When we blow our issues out of proportion, it is much easier to get overwhelmed and stand in our way by feeling sorry for ourselves, intellectualizing the problem, or procrastinating.

Blaming our parents. As anxious attachment forms due to inconsistent parenting, it is easy to shift the blame on our parent or caregiver, often to a point where we create irreconcilable differences or completely distance ourselves from them. It's essential to remember that our parents are imperfect people, constantly battling their unresolved traumas or painful upbringing, and most likely, they did the best they could with their level of awareness and knowledge. Our anxious attachment does not directly reflect on our parents but rather our interpretation of their parenting styles. For example, if our parent was inconsistent with us, it doesn't necessarily mean they did not love us. It could mean several things, from being inexperienced in raising a child to being overwhelmed with other responsibilities.

Giving ourselves a label. With attachment theory, the goal is to identify the cluster of people that needs work in this area. Our attachment explains how we see and deal with difficulties in our lives, mainly in our relationships, depending on the type of care available to us as children. It's nothing more than that. So slapping a label on it is both reductive and detrimental, as we are so much more than just someone who is anxiously attached. Other elements of our personalities play a massive part in how we see the world, and we must consider these to make an informed decision on our life or relationship choices.

Oversimplifying our attachment profile. I often get asked, 'Can I be anxiously and avoidantly attached simultaneously?' and the answer is yes. Our attachment isn't completely black and white, as even though we have a dominant attachment style, we exhibit traits of secure, anxious, and avoidant attachment, depending on our partner, the relationship, the context or the situation, and the people we are around. This mixed attachment profile is very common, and an easy example would be that we might exhibit secure traits around our friends but are anxiously attached to our partners.

Trying to diagnose others. We've all been there. We learned all there is to know about anxious attachment, and now call ourselves pros regarding insecure attachment styles. We look at our friends and potential partners through an attachment lens and label them as 'avoidants' or 'disorganized.' And while it's absolutely okay to wonder about or analyze our friends' or partners' attachment styles, we should not make assumptions based on this, draw consequences about their personalities, or try to predict their future reactions.

THIS IS WHERE YOUR JOURNEY OF SELF-REFLECTION AND HEALING BEGINS. REMEMBER TO STAY CONSISTENT, AND ENJOY THE JOURNEY.

The book is designed to follow a sequence of self-discovery, so try to answer the questions, and do the exercises in the order they come up. There is no good answer to any question, so feel free to write in any shape, form, or length you like. Don't hold back! Write as freely as possible, and remember to enjoy the process.

The questions are categorized to start at the basics; self-reflection, self-discovery, triggers, anxiously attached patterns, etc. As you go on, they will be centered around your relationship habits, insecurities, and how to rewire your old, and dysfunctional dynamics for a better connection. The first part of the workbook will address questions about you, your attachment style, and patterns. The second part is focused on your family, upbringing, and closest relationships with family members and partners. The third part is focused on your relationships, and what role you take in them. If you are single, consider your last relationship, or your ideal future partnership as a frame of reference.

Some of the questions I ask are quite difficult and may provoke sadness, anger, shame, or bad memories to emerge. Practice self-compassion and honesty, and try not to blame or shame yourself for your past mistakes. Remember, our attachment style is not our choice. Most of our anxiously attached behavior happens subconsciously, and it will take consistency and practice to solidify your new patterns. Practice makes better, so do your best to complete this journal and follow up with the suggested exercises.

WHEN DID YOU FIRST BECOME AWARE OF YOUR ANXIOUS ATTACHMENT? HOW DID YOU LEARN ABOUT IT?

_____

_____

_____

_____

_____

_____

_____

WHAT WOULD YOU LIKE TO ACCOMPLISH WITH THE HELP OF THIS JOURNAL? WHAT IS YOUR PRIORITY ON THE HEALING JOURNEY?

_____

_____

_____

_____

_____

_____

_____

HOW DOES ANXIOUS ATTACHMENT DEVELOP?

Anxious attachment develops when a parent or caregiver is inconsistent with their response to a child's emotional needs. This could mean that the caregiver would sometimes be emotionally available to the child while other times, they would be cold and closed off. Children don't fully understand why their parent is giving them inconsistent emotional care and support. Therefore, they grow up fearful that they won't get the emotional support or love needed at any given time and develop coping mechanisms to ensure they stay close to their attachment figures at any cost. It is important to remember that our parents did the best they could for us with the knowledge available to them, at the emotional awareness they had.

Here are a few possible reasons for parent-child misattunement:

➤ The parent is **preoccupied with their problems**, work, or private life and cannot fully devote themselves to the child's needs.

➤ The parent is **confused about the child's needs** and doesn't have a well-developed parenting style.

➤ The parent has **anxiety or depression** and uses the child to console or soothe themselves. This emotional hunger of the caregiver prevents them from focusing on the child's need for love and connection.

➤ The parent has an **anxious attachment style** and is preoccupied with their own triggers and traumas.

➤ The parent (often a single parent) has **unmet emotional needs** and requires the child to fulfill them. In this instance, the roles are often reversed, and the child becomes the parent.

➤ The parent has **substance abuse issues** and is less capable of taking care of their child. They're not as involved or can only show up inconsistently.

➤ The parent believes that **letting the child self-soothe** will benefit them later in life. This parenting technique creates a dynamic where the caregiver is only occasionally available to soothe the child's distress.

➤ The parent **cannot decide on the best parenting practice** and switches between being overly available and not at all. This can make the child confused.

WHO WERE YOU THE CLOSEST TO GROWING UP? WHAT WAS YOUR
RELATIONSHIP LIKE WITH THEM?

_____

_____

_____

_____

_____

_____

_____

WHAT DID YOU LEARN FROM YOUR FAMILY ABOUT EMOTIONS AND
VULNERABILITY? DID YOU MODEL A HEALTHY WAY TO EXPRESS YOUR
FEELINGS AND COMMUNICATE YOUR NEEDS?

_____

_____

_____

_____

_____

_____

DO YOU HAVE A MEMORY FROM YOUR CHILDHOOD THAT YOU REMEMBER TO THIS DAY?

_____

_____

_____

_____

_____

_____

_____

DO YOU THINK THIS MEMORY HAS IMPACTED YOU OR YOUR LIFE? DOES IT REFLECT ON YOUR ADULT RELATIONSHIPS IN ANY WAY?

_____

_____

_____

_____

_____

_____

_____

WHAT TYPE OF PARENT DYNAMIC DID YOU GROW UP WITH?

☐ Parents with a loving, respectful, and low-conflict relationship

☐ Parents with a conflicted relationship, frequent arguments, and dysfunctional ways of communication (blaming, shaming, nitpicking, projecting, etc.)

☐ Parents with a highly dysfunctional marriage, where they use their children as substitutes for one another or love

☐ Overprotective parents and no boundaries in the family

☐ Divorced parents with an amicable relationship

☐ Divorced parents who parted on bad terms, were fighting over custody and it impacted their kids' lives

☐ Single parents with several partners

☐ Single parents who stayed chronically single

☐ One loving and one absent parent

☐ Co-parents, who had a respectful relationship, and prioritized their children

☐ Co-parents with a conflicted relationship

☐ One or both parents were chronically ill and needed to be cared for

☐ Parents with substance abuse issues

☐ One or both parents passed away

☐ Been raised in foster care

IN YOUR OBJECTIVE OPINION, HOW DID YOUR PARENTS RELATE TO EACH OTHER?

_____

_____

_____

_____

_____

_____

_____

DID YOU MODEL HEALTHY PROBLEM SOLVING, COMMUNICATION, AND CONFLICT DE-ESCALATION FROM YOUR PARENTS?

_____

_____

_____

_____

_____

_____

_____

THE MOST COMMON SIGNS OF ANXIOUS ATTACHMENT

Needing constant contact and support from our partner	A constant need for reassurance that we are good enough
Hypersensitivity to rejection and abandonment	Negative self-view and self-worth
Being overly sensitive to other's actions and moods	Difficulty setting boundaries
The impulse to fix, save, or caretake	Being afraid or incapable of being alone
Ruminating and over-analyzing the small things	Catastrophizing
Never saying 'no'	Pretending to be okay
Assuming instead of asking	Developing an over-focus on our partner
Not speaking our needs	Intense jealousy
Manipulative behaviors to keep love in our lives	Putting our partners on a pedestal
Often infringing on the boundaries of others	Thinking we are difficult to handle, needy and high-maintenance

WHAT ARE YOUR MOST PROMINENT ANXIOUSLY ATTACHED TRAITS, AND HOW DO THEY IMPACT YOUR RELATIONSHIPS?

_____

_____

_____

_____

_____

_____

_____

WHAT ARE THE ANXIOUSLY ATTACHED BEHAVIOURS THAT YOU WOULD LIKE TO CHANGE THE MOST?

_____

_____

_____

_____

_____

_____

_____

"HEALING ISN'T ABOUT FILLING YOUR
LIFE WITH UNHEALTHY PLEASURE OR
NEVER HAVING A HARD MOMENT AGAIN.
IT'S ABOUT BEING REAL AND FACING
WHAT YOU FEEL SO THAT IT DOESN'T
ACCUMULATE IN UNHEALTHY WAYS."

YUNG PUEBLO

WHAT DESCRIBES YOU MOST IN A RELATIONSHIP?

- [ ] I often worry about being rejected or abandoned by my partner, even when they continuously reassure me of their love.

- [ ] I fear infidelity, so I look out for cues and monitor my partner's behavior.

- [ ] I want closeness and intimacy in the relationship, but worry whether I can rely on my partner, and if they feel the same way for me.

- [ ] I focus all my energies on my partner to the point that I neglect my own life in the process.

- [ ] I feel threatened, angry, jealous, or worried that my partner no longer wants me when we spend time apart, or when I don't hear from them for what most people would consider a reasonable amount of time.

- [ ] I use certain manipulation techniques to keep my partner close to me; I try to make them feel guilty, jealous, or sorry for me.

- [ ] I overreact to things I see as a threat to the relationship.

- [ ] I try to fix, save, or take care of my partner.

- [ ] I crave constant attention and reassurance from my partner.

- [ ] If I'm in conflict with my partner I cannot think about anything else, but to reestablish the connection with them.

- [ ] I resort to protest behaviors to get my partner's attention when in conflict; I pick fights with them, give them the silent treatment, or avoid them to get their attention.

- [ ] I constantly fear I'm not good enough for my partner.

THE MOST PROMINENT ANXIOUS ATTACHMENT TRAITS IN RELATIONSHIPS

We exhibit specific unconscious behaviors in relationships to stay close to our partners and maintain our 'importance' in their lives. These behaviors are coping mechanisms developed in early childhood and can be the result of the internalized shame of 'not being good enough,' of not learning healthy communication techniques in our childhood, and of not knowing how to express our feelings.

We are clingy. To be clingy means to stay highly close to or dependent on someone for emotional support and a sense of security. This means we need constant contact and reassurance to feel connected to our partner. This often means we disrespect our partner's boundaries or make them feel bad for taking time out of the relationship.

We can get irrationally jealous. Jealousy is part of life; a healthy amount comes up even in secure relationships. But with anxious attachment, we can be so preoccupied with the availability of our partner that we pay too much attention to their patterns and can become irrationally jealous if we find something out of character. Research has found that people's attachment styles influence how they experience jealousy in their partnerships. Anxiously attached people experience more anger and irritability. They are more likely to engage in surveillance behavior and are hypervigilant to cues of rejection or perceived threats to their relationship.

We often micromanage our partners' lives in an effort to make ourselves invaluable and a 'great asset' to the relationship. This also gives us a sense of control over our partnerships, predicting the outcome of most situations and making us feel safer and more secure in the relationship.

We go from 0 to 100 in a matter of minutes. We've all experienced problems that were so overwhelming that we just couldn't control our reaction and let things get out of hand pretty quickly. This is very common for the anxiously attached, for we didn't learn to effectively regulate our own emotions and soothe ourselves as children. We grew up in a constant turbulence of emotions and have learned that ups and downs are normal. At the same time, we have a lot of underlying anger, frustration, and resentment, and these resurface when our core wound gets triggered.

We assume the roles of savior, fixer, and caretaker. Trying to help others is natural and can come from a place of good, but with anxious attachment, we often try to save people from their own problems. We unconsciously try to prove our worth in a relationship; therefore, we choose people who we can save, fix, or who need taking care of. This can get to a point where we are more focused on fixing our person than accepting and loving them for who they are.

We believe that we need to work hard to be loved. If we grew up thinking that love is conditional, then we likely learned to audition or work hard to get it. This behavior is carried into our adult relationships, where we tend to think we need to earn our partner's love and affection. That's why we often end up putting more effort into our partnerships than our significant others.

We show manipulative behaviors. Those of us with anxious attachment are more likely to engage in manipulative behaviors to prevent our partner from leaving the relationship. We may also use manipulative techniques to have our needs met or control the outcome of certain situations. These can look like gaslighting our partner, stonewalling, or threatening to leave the relationship when we have no intention to do so.

WHAT ARE THE ANXIOUS TRAITS THAT HAVE THE MOST PROFOUND IMPACT ON YOUR RELATIONSHIPS AND WHY?

_____

_____

_____

_____

_____

_____

_____

WHAT ARE THE MOST SIGNIFICANT BEHAVIOURS THAT YOU WANT TO SHARE WITH YOUR PARTNER?

_____

_____

_____

_____

_____

_____

_____

WHAT IS SECURE ATTACHMENT IN A RELATIONSHIP?

When aiming for secure attachment, we must first understand what it is and how it influences our relationships. **Securely attached relationships build on understanding and meeting one another's needs, working towards supporting the partner while allowing them to be their authentic self.** In secure relationships, the partners rely on and support each other without becoming codependent. They develop problem-solving strategies, de-escalating and reconnecting after a fight, and work towards long-term relationship satisfaction. As securely attached people grow up modeling a positive caregiver relationship, they can replicate a healthy connection with others in all types of relationships. Securely attached people are more social, warm, and easy to connect to. They are in touch with and can express their feelings. They can build deep, meaningful, and long-lasting relationships with others.

Securely attached people are:

➢ Able to demonstrate **healthy emotional regulation** in a relationship; they are more likely to remain calm when triggered and respond rather than react
➢ Able to **plan and think about long-term goals** with their partner
➢ Great at bonding, **opening up to, and trusting others,** as well as letting others in, actively listening to them, and offering support
➢ Good at **communicating their needs effectively,** respecting the needs of their partner, and less likely to trespass on their boundaries
➢ Comfortable with **closeness and mutual dependency,** aren't afraid to ask for or provide help to their partner without pushing in on them or becoming overbearing
➢ Actively **seeking emotional support** from their partner and offering emotional support in return
➢ **Comfortable being alone** or giving their partner time alone when needed
➢ **Able to reflect on how they act in a relationship**, what mistakes they make, and are willing to offer an apology or resolution to problems when needed
➢ Actively **working towards mutual relational satisfaction,** by allowing their partner to be their authentic self, express their needs, set healthy boundaries, and find mutual ground in problem-solving

WHAT IS YOUR DEFINITION OF A HEALTHY, LOVING RELATIONSHIP?

_____

_____

_____

_____

_____

_____

_____

HOW DO YOU LIKE TO GIVE AND RECEIVE LOVE?

_____

_____

_____

_____

_____

_____

_____

WHAT IS THE MOST IMPORTANT TO YOU IN A RELATIONSHIP?

☐	Accountability	☐	Flexibility
☐	Vulnerability	☐	Commitment
☐	Kindness	☐	Safety
☐	Intimacy	☐	Quality time
☐	Reliability	☐	Effort
☐	Self-awareness	☐	Empathy
☐	Loyalty	☐	Trust
☐	Honesty	☐	Support
☐	Shared values	☐	Healthy communication
☐	Shared interests	☐	Consistency
☐	Humour	☐	Understanding

WHAT QUALITIES ARE YOU LOOKING FOR IN A PARTNER?

_____

_____

_____

_____

_____

_____

_____

WHAT ARE YOUR NON-NEGOTIABLES IN A PARTNERSHIP?

_____

_____

_____

_____

_____

_____

_____

SELF-LOVE AND SELF-ESTEEM

The concept of self-love can be fleeting for most of us. We think, 'Oh, but I like myself,' while we have a variety of ways we betray our trust, sabotage our relationships, and overstep our boundaries. **In essence, self-love means having a high regard for our well-being and happiness. It means taking care of our needs and not sacrificing ourselves to please others.** Self-love means not settling for less than we deserve, prioritizing and trusting ourselves, talking about ourselves positively, setting healthy boundaries, and learning to forgive our mistakes.

Ways to practice self-love include:

Becoming mindful. It translates into being able to tune into what we think and how we feel at the present moment without giving in to any interruptions around us. It is shown to have many benefits, from balancing our mood to reducing stress levels.

Practicing self-care. It is proven that people who take better care of themselves report higher overall satisfaction in their lives and relationships. Good self-care habits include healthy nutrition, regular physical exercise, healthy social life, and proper sleep.

Opting for healthy choices. By opting for healthy choices, you encourage yourself to value your needs and start looking at yourself as a high-value person. This can be anything from choosing a healthy home-cooked meal over take-out to saying no to inconsistent dating patterns.

Learning to say 'no'. With anxious attachment, we dismiss our feelings, minimize our problems, and neglect to express our needs out of fear of coming across as needy or high-maintenance. So learning to say 'no' to things we don't want to allow into our lives or that we don't have the emotional or mental capacity for will be a crucial part of the healing process.

This might sound overwhelming initially, but cognitive behavioral therapy tells us that if we fear something and expose ourselves to it repeatedly, we will gradually learn that nothing terrible will happen to us. Moreover, we'll eventually see the situation as safe and become desensitized to the threat. So if saying 'no' feels threatening, try taking baby steps by drawing healthy boundaries around the request.

➤ "I would love to help you with this, but I don't have the time this week. If that works for you, I can manage a few hours next week."

➤ "I would love to join you, but I won't be able to stay very long."

➤ "I'm not comfortable spending a whole weekend with your family. Could we work out something else instead? Perhaps a family dinner next week?"

➤ "I don't have the emotional capacity to discuss this now, but I would love to help you out some other way."

Getting into the practice of meeting our own needs. Meeting our needs sounds profound, yet many of us dismiss our own needs and wants 'in the interest of the relationship.' So a great way to shift this in the right direction is to ask yourself, "What do I need right now? What could I do for myself or give myself to feel better in this situation?" And the answer might be much simpler than you think. It could be some time alone, a nice bubble bath, a healthy home-cooked meal, or regular yoga or fitness classes. Paying attention to our bodies and re-learning to be in tune with ourselves will tremendously impact our lives and partnerships.

Purging toxic relationships and behavior from our lives. Work to reduce the times you are subjected to anything that triggers you or sends your nervous system into fight or flight mode. The easiest way to achieve this in your romantic life is to date securely attached people; however, this isn't always possible. So work to reduce the times you get triggered by recognizing what triggers you and laying clear and firm boundaries around this behavior. Let your partner know what is and isn't acceptable and what you need to stay safe and reassured in the relationship.

Also, pay attention to your reactions in triggering situations and learn to recognize them when they happen so that you can leave and self-regulate. Work to limit your time around people or situations that trigger you. For example, if you find your partner's friends or family upsetting, limit your contact or time with them. Putting your own mental health and well-being first might feel selfish at the beginning, especially if you are used to sacrificing your own needs in the interest of others, so again, take baby steps.

WHY DO YOU THINK YOU ARE A GREAT PARTNER? WHY WOULD YOU CHOOSE YOURSELF?

_____

_____

_____

_____

_____

_____

_____

WHAT WOULD YOU LIKE TO CHANGE IN YOURSELF TO CULTIVATE A HEALTHY CONNECTION?

_____

_____

_____

_____

_____

_____

_____

DO YOU COMPARE YOURSELF TO OTHERS? DO OTHER PEOPLE'S LOOKS, ACCOMPLISHMENTS, OR LIVES MAKE YOU INSECURE?

_____

_____

_____

_____

_____

_____

_____

CAN YOU FIND YOUR WORTH BEHIND EVERY INSECURITY? CAN YOU REASSURE YOURSELF OF YOUR OWN QUALITIES AND VALUES?

_____

_____

_____

_____

_____

_____

_____

RECURRING PATTERNS IN RELATIONSHIPS

With anxious attachment, reviewing how it all started, how our core wound was created, and how we carried this wound through our adult relationships is helpful. **We all have recurring patterns that relate to our attachment style, indicating attachment wounds throughout our entire dating history.** That's why it's vital to take a moment and review what is the recurring theme we carry from partnership to partnership. This could be anything from being clingy, habitually overstepping our partner's boundaries, being fixated on the speed with which our partner responds to our texts, being overly agreeable, or acting out of jealousy.

In essence, a relationship pattern is repeating the same behaviors over and over again with new people in our lives. We can exhibit these patterns in romantic relationships, friendships, and work relationships.

They indicate three main things:

➤ **Who do we get into relationships with,** do we choose the same type of person, and if so, why
➤ **Our interactions with them**, the behaviors we exhibit around them while in the relationship, common protest behaviors, communication techniques, expression of needs, and boundaries
➤ **How do we let them treat us**, what do we allow them to do, and how do we allow these people to treat us in the partnership

To identify your recurring patterns try to work backward and examine your current or past relationships. Examine your role in the dynamic and your partner's role. Is there a recurring theme? Do you keep repeating the same behavior? Do you recognize the same scenarios or relational dynamic play out in each instance with a different partner? Work to identify the most common recurring patterns in your current and past relationships.

➤ "If I feel emotional distance from my partner, I become unsure of my value and project my insecurities on my partner by picking fights."

➤ "I am scared that my partner will leave me, so I encourage them to put themselves first in the partnership while I neglect myself."

CAN YOU SPOT A PATTERN IN WHO YOU USUALLY DATE, OR HOW YOUR RELATIONSHIP UNFOLDS WITH THEM?

_____

_____

_____

_____

_____

_____

_____

WHERE DO YOUR MOST PROMINENT RECURRING PATTERNS COME FROM? ARE YOU MODELING YOUR PARENTS' RELATIONSHIP? DO THESE PATTERNS REFLECT A CORE WOUND?

_____

_____

_____

_____

_____

_____

_____

HOW DO WE COMMUNICATE WITH ANXIOUS ATTACHMENT?

Our earliest experience with relationships is witnessing our parents or caregivers being in one. This forms our view of what a relationship dynamic looks like, even if this dynamic is not the healthiest. We soak up our parents' communication styles, expressions of mood, body language, and how they relate to one another. We learn – or don't – how relationships work through our parents. We develop several communication techniques, some of which can erode our partnerships in the long run.

With anxious attachment, we use a number of these dysfunctional communication techniques, and very often, we don't realize how they impact the narrative of what we are trying to relay or the dynamic between us and our partner. Anxiously attached people are generally open and willing to share vulnerably with their partners. They don't have problems opening up to discuss relationship issues; they prefer solving them rather than letting things fester. However, they don't always choose the best tools to express their distress or ask for their needs or wants. Here are some of the most common dysfunctional communication techniques that come up for a lot of us:

Criticizing
Criticizing our partners when they can't meet our emotional needs is very common in anxious attachment communication. We do this to avoid coming across as needy or demanding. Instead of communicating the real problem, we deflect and start bringing up our partner's faults or past mistakes in both big and small ways. Through criticizing, we unconsciously try to let our partner know that we need more attention, reassurance, or validation.

Being needy
We tend to be clingy and needy in relationships as a way to get closer to our partners. We call and text them excessively to establish a connection, and this gets pushed to unhealthy extremes. This usually happens when we feel that our partner either emotionally or physically pulls away. We go into a panicked frenzy, not knowing how to reconnect. So we smother them in attention instead of asking for the reason for the disconnect or giving them space to regulate their emotions.

Nitpicking

Nitpicking is the tendency to look for minor faults or mistakes in our partners and bring them up in response to a situation we can't or don't want to address directly. For example, we are arguing with our partners over something we asked them to do. We can't seem to get our way because the partner is unresponsive or unwilling to solve the problem, so instead of expressing how disappointed we are, we start bringing up their faults or past mistakes.

Stonewalling

This happens when in a discussion or argument, one partner withdraws from the conversation, shutting down and physically or mentally distancing themselves from the other. This might be their response to feeling overwhelmed; metaphorically speaking, they pull up a wall around them. Stonewalling can show up by giving the silent treatment, rolling the eyes, looking away from the partner, acting busy, and ignoring the conversation altogether.

Shaming

By shaming, we try to make our partners look bad and shift the blame, suggesting they are the problem, not us. Shaming can come out in many forms, from calling the partner too dramatic, too needy, or having little empathy to directly shaming them in front of friends or family by calling attention to something they lack or did wrong.

Projecting

Projecting is a defensive technique we use to project traits or habits we don't like in ourselves to our partner. This works like taking our problem or insecurity and making it sound like our partner's fault. It can sound like, "You are the problem, not me," or "You probably cheated on me; that's why you act weird."

Deflecting

Deflecting means consistently distracting from the problem and shifting blame to the partner. Deflecting is a way to avoid the negative consequences of any actions while blaming others. Deflecting can feel dismissive and inconsiderate as the partner who engages in this technique minimizes the other's feelings, steering away from dealing with the problem at hand.

Keeping score

We keep score to avoid addressing issues and shift the blame onto the partner by putting one on them. In the heat of the argument, we often don't respond to the topic at hand but bring up something painful the partner did to us.

WHICH TYPE OF COMMUNICATION DID YOU OBSERVE GROWING UP?

Open, honest, and healthy communication, respecting each other's boundaries	Taking accountability for words, actions, and reactions
Constantly criticising the partner	Giving the silent treatment
Nitpicking the partner	Shaming and blaming one another
Didn't see them communicate with each other or solve problems together	Deflecting one's own faults
Projecting one's mistakes and insecurities	Keeping score of each other's faults and mistakes
Stonewalling: shutting down, cold-shouldering the partner, eye-rolling	Freezing in the face of a problem

CAN YOU RECOGNISE ANY OF THESE PATTERNS IN YOUR OWN
RELATIONSHIPS?

_____

_____

_____

_____

_____

_____

_____

CAN YOU RECALL ANY INSTANCE WHEN DYSFUNCTIONAL COMMUNICATION
LEAD TO BREAKING UP YOUR RELATIONSHIP?

_____

_____

_____

_____

_____

_____

_____

SELF-REGULATION AND SELF-AWARENESS

These are robust tools we need to learn to start reparenting ourselves. **Self-awareness is our ability to notice how our actions, thoughts, or emotions do or don't align with our inner self.** If we are self-aware, we can objectively evaluate ourselves, align our behavior with our values, and understand how others perceive us. **In comparison, self-regulation is the ability to control our emotions and the actions we take in response to them, considering what is appropriate for each situation.**

The ability to self-regulate is vital in successfully creating and maintaining healthy relationships. **Not many people know that our ability to control our emotions and how we respond to them is influenced by our attachment style.** While it's important to understand when to trust our emotions, it's equally important to know how our attachment style impacts how we self-regulate. Self-regulation is learned in early childhood through our primary caregivers, who teach us how to downregulate negative and upregulate positive emotions. If co-regulation doesn't happen, we must learn emotional grounding techniques to regulate our nervous system in our adult years.

WHAT IS EMOTIONAL REGULATION?

Emotional regulation is the process by which we can influence what emotions we have when we have them, and how we experience or express our feelings to others. On a day-to-day basis, we face hundreds of stimuli, and it's unavoidable that some of them are negative. That is when emotional regulation comes into the picture. It acts as a modifier, and it helps us filter these stimuli and respond to them in a way that doesn't evoke stress or fear.

Several studies suggest that people with poor emotional regulation strategies are more likely to fall prey to their circumstances and their feelings by not being able to control how they act or react in certain situations. In essence, emotional regulation allows us to determine the outcomes of certain triggering instances by helping us balance and judge what is appropriate for the situation and what isn't. **Emotional regulation is about pausing between the feeling and the reaction, and the more effective we become at creating a distance, the better we'll be able to understand and communicate our feelings.**

HOW TO GET STARTED WITH REGULATING OUR EMOTIONS?

To master emotional regulation, we first have to get curious about our feelings that come up in triggering situations. Then we need to find a way to sit in the discomfort of negative emotions and release them. Then as a final step, we have to get curious about what core wound the feeling indicates.

➤ Notice yourself getting worked up, getting disappointed, or feeling let down.

➤ Pay attention to your fears and core needs in a relationship. Do you fear infidelity? Are you afraid of being rejected? Do you need constant reassurance from your partner?

➤ Observe your thoughts as they come up without attaching any shame, blame, or meaning to them. Instead, reflect to find out the emotions it brings up in you

➤ Don't react to these emotions, try to sit with them instead. Feel them and let them pass. It's completely okay to cry, yell, punch a pillow, push against the wall to release tension, jump up and down, or shake your arms.

➤ Now get curious! What are the more subtle feelings behind the primary emotion? Can you identify them? Can you connect them to an age or a past situation? Use the emotional wheel to identify the feelings!

➤ Once you identify the anxious feelings and core wounds, challenge them. Ask yourself if they are your reality, reflect your worth, or are internalized feelings or thoughts from childhood. This can look like asking yourself the following questions:

Is this about my relationship, or is it connected to a deep-rooted insecurity?

Do I really feel unlovable, or did I learn to put myself last as a child?

Does my partner's behavior reflect on me, or is it simply their way of dealing with conflict?

Challenging your thoughts and automatic reactions will open up a new perspective, help you see a different version of the same story, and make you more accepting of yourself and others.

According to research, humans experience two types of emotions; primary and secondary. **Primary emotions** are the first to come up when we face a new situation, and they are grouped into four pairs of polar opposites: joy-sadness, anger-fear, trust-disgust, and surprise-anticipation.

Secondary emotions are felt when the primary ones wear off, and can often be habitual or learned responses. They are more nuanced and can influence our behavior, increase the intensity of our reactions, and usually last longer than primary emotions.

The below emotional wheel can help you identify your more nuanced feelings.

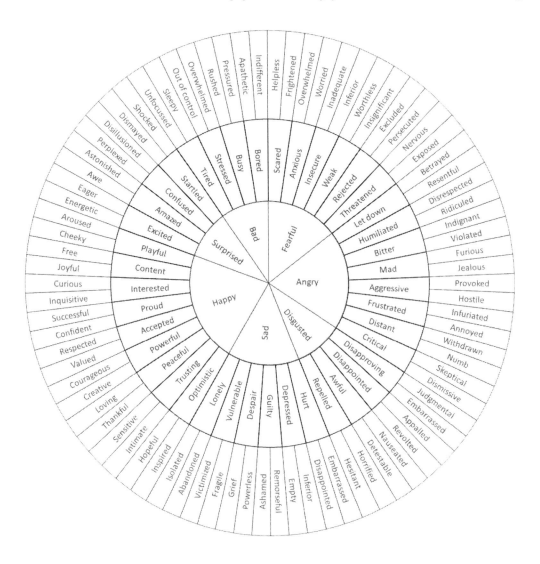

DID YOU HAVE A GREAT SUPPORT SYSTEM OF FAMILY AND FRIENDS GROWING UP? WHO DID YOU TURN TO WHEN IN DISTRESS OR NEED?

_____

_____

_____

_____

_____

_____

CAN YOU SOOTHE YOURSELF WHEN TRIGGERED? OR DO YOU NEED VALIDATION, REASSURANCE, AND COMFORTING FROM SOMEONE ELSE?

_____

_____

_____

_____

_____

_____

CAN YOU RECALL A PAST SITUATION WHEN YOU SUCCESSFULLY REGULATED YOURSELF IN THE FACE OF A TRIGGER? HOW?

_____

_____

_____

_____

_____

_____

_____

TRY TO RECALL A SITUATION THAT CONSTANTLY TRIGGERS YOU. HOW CAN YOU SOOTHE YOURSELF IF IT HAPPENS AGAIN?

_____

_____

_____

_____

_____

_____

_____

CAN YOU ACCEPT HELP PRAISE OR COMPLIMENTS FROM OTHERS WITHOUT DEFLECTING OR INSTANTLY RETURNING THEM?

_____

_____

_____

_____

_____

_____

_____

WHAT ARE THE QUALITIES YOU REALLY LIKE ABOUT YOURSELF? HOW COULD YOU REMIND YOURSELF OF THEM ON A DAILY/WEEKLY BASIS?

_____

_____

_____

_____

_____

_____

_____

WHAT IS A CORE WOUND

A core wound is something that many of us carry with us throughout our lives. **It's an emotional wound that we form from the suppressed pain that we experienced in childhood.** These wounds can be challenging to heal, but it's essential to recognize them and work through them to move forward and live a fulfilling life. Whether through therapy, self-reflection, or other methods, addressing our core wounds can help us break free from negative patterns and live more authentically. Core wounds can be the byproduct of abandonment, bullying, neglect, inconsistencies, invalidation, gaslighting, or abuse.

Core wounds run deep and get triggered by adult experiences, primarily relational experiences. They defy intellect, so while our thinking brains are aware of our worth and we know that we feel disproportionately about these, we still can't help them. **Core wounds create limiting beliefs in us that 'serve' to reaffirm our core beliefs about ourselves.** These can sound like "I'm not good enough to deserve a better relationship." or "I need to fit in to be accepted." Let's have a look at the most relevant core wounding with anxious attachment.

The rejection core wound develops from instances when our parent pushes away or ignores us. This might mean that we are actively dating people who end up ghosting us or ditching abruptly with no warning. This core wound results in the need for attention, the need to be seen and heard. It can cause us to become clingy and needy of our partner, sometimes demanding.

With this core wound, we feel that we are not enough, we do not count, or we are overlooked; even in a loving relationship and with a supportive partner, this core wound gets triggered every time we feel overlooked, ignored, or not chosen.

The abandonment wound develops if your parent was inconsistent, unpredictable, or absent. This might mean that in your adult relationships, you choose people who make you constantly worry that they will abandon you too. The abandonment wound results in the need for affection, a need to connect to someone else, to belong, and to create a connection. This is often why we attach prematurely to partners, put them on a pedestal, and refuse to see their red flags until too late. We desperately need to be chosen by our person. We feel that we are not connected; we are not loved.

The enmeshment core wound develops when the boundaries between the child and parent are blurred, or simply nonexistent. This might contribute to you ending up in relationships where your identity is completely absorbed into your partner's, where you constantly cater to their needs, losing your sense of personality and neglecting your own needs. It results in a sense of timidness in relationships, starting to act, react, feel, and behave like the partner. With this wound, there is a need to feel accepted, be similar to, or want similar things to the partner.

The shame core wound develops when you grow up facing constant shaming or criticism from a caregiver. You may internalize this as you are inherently bad or flawed. This shows up in your adult relationships by mainly opting for partners who reinforce this belief system, helping it to set in even more. It's a catch-22 where your partners will continually reaffirm this core belief, pushing you further into believing that something is wrong with you, so you keep choosing partners who reaffirm this, helping the negative belief set in even further.

The helplessness core wound develops when we are left to fend for ourselves, as our caregiver isn't available to tend to our immediate needs. When we needed help, soothing, or reassurance as children, nobody was coming to our aid, and we felt powerless. This core wound results in a deep need for approval, often paired with self-hatred. This wound makes us feel like we are not good enough, are not competent, will never achieve our goals, or are a failure. Someone with this core wound may need a lot of reassurance and may outsource all the validation for their decisions or life choices to their friends, family members, or romantic partners.

Parentification happens when a child is made to feel responsible for the emotional or physical needs of their parent or caregiver. This can lead to wanting to save, fix, or caretake partners in our adult relationships, neglecting our wellbeing. This happens because we unconsciously feel the need to replicate and resolve our past issues. The roles of fixer, savior, and caretaker are typical manifestations of the parentification wound but are mainly aimed at trying to control the outcome of certain situations to feel safe in the relationship.

The mistrust wound develops when the caregiver is abusive or neglectful towards the child, leading to feelings of skepticism and suspicion in adult relationships. With this core wound, you might end up dating people who prove this distrust well-founded, creating a self-fulfilling prophecy and solidifying this belief system.

HAVE YOU ADOPTED ANY OF THE FOLLOWING LIMITING BELIEFS?

- [ ] I'm not good enough, so I focus on other people instead of myself

- [ ] No one will ever love me with my insecurities and neediness

- [ ] I must do everything in my power to please my partner because that's normal

- [ ] I need to do more, or I will be abandoned

- [ ] I can't hold onto a healthy relationship

- [ ] I've always been this way and I can't change it

- [ ] Others will love me back, I just need to love them enough

- [ ] I always make a mess of everything, there is something wrong with me

- [ ] My clinginess pushes potential partners away

- [ ] I need to hide certain aspects of my personality to be accepted

- [ ] I can't trust myself to do the right thing

- [ ] I feel worthless without validation and reassurance from my partner

- [ ] I am not enough when I'm not in a relationship

- [ ] I must save, fix, or take care of people in order for them to love me

- [ ] If I speak my needs I will be judged and rejected

- [ ] I must make decisions in order to avoid being abandoned and rejected

LIST OUT ALL YOUR LIMITING BELIEFS INCLUDING ALL THE NEGATIVE INNER CHATTER YOU HAVE.

_____

_____

_____

_____

_____

_____

_____

CAN YOU CONNECT THESE LIMITING BELIEFS TO A PAST EXPERIENCE? DO THEY REFLECT ON YOUR CURRENT SELF?

_____

_____

_____

_____

_____

_____

_____

WHAT IS YOUR BIGGEST INSECURITY YOU CAN'T SEEM TO SHAKE OFF? DO
YOU REMEMBER WHERE IT STEMS FROM? IF YOU WERE TO OBJECTIVELY
QUESTION IT, WOULD IT BE TRUE?

_____

_____

_____

_____

_____

_____

HAS THIS INSECURITY EVER HELD YOU BACK FROM SHARING YOURSELF
AUTHENTICALLY, OPENING UP, OR GETTING YOUR NEEDS MET IN A
RELATIONSHIP?

_____

_____

_____

_____

_____

HOW DO YOU COPE WITH PAINFUL SITUATIONS OR EMOTIONAL HURT?

_____

_____

_____

_____

_____

_____

_____

_____

HOW DOES SPENDING TIME ALONE MAKE YOU FEEL?

_____

_____

_____

_____

_____

_____

_____

_____

HAVE YOU EVER GIVEN UP ANY ASPECT OF YOUR LIFE (FRIENDS, HOBBIES, ROUTINES) BECAUSE YOU STARTED A RELATIONSHIP WITH SOMEONE?

_____

_____

_____

_____

_____

_____

_____

HOW CAN YOU PRIORITISE YOURSELF IN A RELATIONSHIP WITHOUT FEELING GUILTY, OR FEARFUL OF ABANDONMENT?

_____

_____

_____

_____

_____

_____

_____

WHICH OF THESE APPLY TO YOU THE MOST IN RELATIONSHIPS?

☐ I'm always the first to offer a solution to any problem

☐ I often catch myself giving people unsolicited advice, instead of listening to them

☐ I am drawn to people who need saving, fixing, or taking care of

☐ I assume most of the household responsibilities

☐ I often feel resentful for being the audience or therapist to others

☐ I don't talk a lot about my needs, nor do I share my thoughts

☐ I say 'yes' even when I mean to say 'no'

☐ I often feel mentally exhausted to meet people and avoid going out

☐ I have the feeling I know my partner better than they know me

☐ I give more in the relationship than I receive

☐ People always rely on me for help, advice, or a sympathetic ear

☐ I hardly have time for my own life, friends, family, or hobbies

☐ I often feel that I'm neglecting my own career in order to be a better partner

☐ I don't feel that I'm getting my needs met in my relationship

☐ I'm scared that saying 'no' will influence my partner's feelings for me

☐ I shy away from showing my authentic self because I fear being judged

WHAT IS PEOPLE-PLEASING?

People pleasing is a learned behavior we employ to keep love in our lives and keep the connection alive with our parent, caretaker, or significant other. **People-pleasing means doing things for others at our own expense, things that are outside our reach or comfort zone, or simply not our responsibility to handle.**

As it is initially an automatic response, this protective strategy begins primarily outside of our awareness. However, over time, it may become one of our strategies to protect ourselves when we feel unsafe emotionally or relationally. It makes sense to try and please the person you feel threatened by or with whom you want to build a connection. However, if it becomes how you handle almost everything over time, it may impact your happiness, physical well-being, and relationship satisfaction.

What people-pleasing looks like in a relationship context:

➤ You don't express your feelings if you think this will negatively impact your relationship
➤ You find it difficult to ask for help or accept help
➤ You take over the responsibilities of others even when you can hardly handle your own
➤ You say 'yes' even when you mean to say 'no'
➤ You don't express your needs or communicate your boundaries
➤ You are unable to make decisions on your own because you fear the outcome will negatively impact others
➤ You rarely consider your happiness, putting others first
➤ You fix other people's problems, try to save them, and be their caretaker
➤ You assume roles in people's lives, overstepping healthy boundaries to please or save them
➤ You are preoccupied with what other people might think of you
➤ You apologize for everything
➤ You pretend to agree with people, even when you have a different opinion

People-pleasing can backfire in many ways. Putting all your effort into keeping others happy can deplete your resources, not to mention taking away time and energy from tackling your own goals or facing your challenges. People-pleasers often put their own life on the back burner to accommodate others.

HOW TO STOP PEOPLE-PLEASING?

People-pleasing has been ingrained in most of us, and in the long run, it may leave us feeling depleted and unhappy. Not to mention that it builds up resentment in us, impacting relational satisfaction and our connection with our partner. So here are a few ways to turn this around and shift the focus back on yourself.

Recognize your needs, make yourself a priority, and work to meet your needs rather than focusing all your energies on others. Working to recognize what you need to feel complete and safe will help take the pressure off of keeping others satisfied, not to mention that it can increase relational satisfaction.

Set boundaries with others as well as yourself. This might be a difficult one, but learning to say 'no' will help you reprioritize your own life and set a healthy boundary with others. Internalize that it isn't selfish to set boundaries. It is merely self-protection.

Assess the request. Take your time to determine whether you have the resources to help, and most importantly, whether you want to. Remember, declining and focusing on your own life isn't selfish. In fact, the more content and fulfilled you are, the more you can contribute to others' happiness.

Learn to sit in the discomfort of change. When you spend your life pleasing others and outsourcing your powers, it will feel incredibly selfish to say 'no' for the first time. So learn to sit with the feeling, without blaming or shaming yourself. Accept that people might be disappointed when you are longer available, and that is okay!

Take your time with responding. This will buy you extra time, with which you can reflect and decide. Learn not to say 'yes' to everything instantly. Take your time, and create a little distance between yourself and the request. This can help you assess whether you actually have the resources to help and can help make the right choice.

Take baby steps. People-pleasing is a difficult habit to change, so if you find it hard to say 'no' or set firm boundaries, take baby steps. This can look like not volunteering to help with something, or learning to accept help from others.

"SEPARATE YOUR WORTH FROM THE APPROVAL OF OTHERS. YOUR GOAL IN LIFE IS NOT TO BE LIKED AND VALIDATED BY OTHERS. FOCUS ON ACCEPTING ALL OF YOURSELF INCLUDING THE PARTS THAT YOU ARE HEALING."

YOUR RELATIONSHIP RESET

WHAT ARE YOUR MOST PROMINENT PEOPLE-PLEASING TENDENCIES?

_____

_____

_____

_____

_____

_____

_____

HAVE YOU EVER OVERSTEPPED YOUR BOUNDARIES BECAUSE OF AN OVER-FOCUS ON YOUR PARTNER?

_____

_____

_____

_____

_____

_____

_____

IN WHAT WAYS DO YOU TEND TO NEGLECT YOURSELF OR YOUR OWN NEEDS
IN A RELATIONSHIP?

_____

_____

_____

_____

_____

_____

_____

CAN YOU IDENTIFY BEHAVIOURS THAT CHANGE WHEN YOU ARE IN A
RELATIONSHIP, COMPARED TO WHEN YOU ARE SINGLE?

_____

_____

_____

_____

_____

_____

_____

HOW COULD YOU STAY CONNECTED TO YOURSELF AND YOUR LIFE IN A RELATIONSHIP? WHAT DO YOU WANT TO HOLD SPACE FOR?

_____

_____

_____

_____

_____

_____

_____

WHAT BOUNDARIES COULD YOU SET WITH YOURSELF TO PROTECT YOUR RESOURCES AND REPRIORITISE YOURSELF?

_____

_____

_____

_____

_____

_____

_____

WHAT IS A TRIGGER?

Emotional triggers can be anything that causes our mind and body to react in extreme and unexpected ways, regardless of our current mood. This can include experiences, events, people, places, or things. Each triggering experience is different, determined by what causes it. A trigger can be anything that causes us to recall a traumatic experience from our past. Some common situations that cause us anxious attachers to get triggered are rejection, betrayal, being excluded or ignored, feeling unwanted, or losing a connection. It is important to mention that anxious attachers may get triggered by the perceived threat of any of the above situations. For example, our partner is asking for space, and based on our childhood experiences of neglect, we instantly jump to the conclusion that they don't love, care for, or want to be with us anymore.

HOW TO RECOGNIZE YOUR TRIGGERS?

The easiest way to recognize our triggers is to pay attention to situations that generate strong emotions or bodily sensations. Emotional sensations might be crying, unexplained anger, panic, sadness, or emptiness. Physical sensations include a pounding heart, ˜sweaty hands, dizziness, numbness, or upset stomach. If these arise unexpectedly in situations, and we cannot explain why they're there, we have a good reason to believe that our attachment trauma or a core wound is triggering us. Some of the most common anxiously attached triggers are:

➢ Partner needing **space or time alone**, away from us
➢ **Inconsistent behavior** we pick up on in the relationship
➢ Partner being **emotionally closed off**
➢ **Refusal to commit** or solve problems together
➢ Physical distance
➢ **Mixed signals**
➢ Lack of open communication or transparency
➢ **Secrets in the relationship**
➢ Partner is not willing to share their feelings
➢ Partner having interests outside of the relationship, that make us feel excluded
➢ **Focus shifting outside the relationship**

WHAT PHYSICAL SENSATIONS AND URGES DO YOU FEEL WHEN YOU'RE TRIGGERED?

- [ ] I feel numb in part or my entire body

- [ ] I get a headache or migraine

- [ ] I feel faint and dizzy

- [ ] I feel nauseous and my stomach is upset

- [ ] My heart is racing

- [ ] I have breathing difficulties

- [ ] I start sweating excessively

- [ ] I cannot seem to focus on anything

- [ ] I get restless or start fidgeting

- [ ] I unconsciously start shaking my leg

- [ ] I feel a knot in my throat or stomach

- [ ] My muscles go stiff

- [ ] I space out, becoming unaware of my surroundings

- [ ] I feel a sudden urge to go to the toilet

- [ ] I lose my voice

- [ ] I start tapping with my fingers or feet unconsciously

TRY TO REMEMBER A SITUATION WHERE YOU WERE TRIGGERED. WHAT
HAPPENED? WHAT DID IT FEEL LIKE?

_____

_____

_____

_____

_____

_____

_____

CAN YOU REMEMBER A TRIGGERING SITUATION THAT YOU MANAGED TO
OVERCOME? WHAT DID YOU DO?

_____

_____

_____

_____

_____

_____

_____

WHAT CAN YOU 'RECYCLE' FROM THIS REACTION? HOW CAN YOU REPEAT
THIS THE NEXT TIME YOU'RE TRIGGERED?

_____

_____

_____

_____

_____

_____

_____

HOW DO YOU SOOTHE YOURSELF IN DIFFICULT SITUATIONS?

_____

_____

_____

_____

_____

_____

_____

EMOTIONAL GROUNDING TECHNIQUES

Emotional grounding techniques are widely recommended by therapists and coaches to help their clients navigate dissociation or overwhelm. When a strong reaction kicks in, we can start spacing out, leaving our bodies and getting worked up, feeling like we are not in control anymore. That's when these techniques come in handy because they can help pull us away from flashbacks, unwanted memories, or negative emotions. **Grounding techniques help us refocus on the present moment and distract ourselves from our anxious thoughts and feelings.** There are several methods, from journaling, yoga, EFT tapping, belly breathing, and meditation to simply putting your hands under cold water. Let's go through the most effective exercises.

Journaling

You might remember keeping a diary from your teenage years, a place to jot down your struggles and fears without judgment. The concept and benefits of journaling as an adult are the same. By writing down your thoughts and feelings, you achieve clarity and create distance between intrusive thoughts and reality. With anxious attachment, it can be a fantastic tool to write down your anxious 'episodes' whenever you get triggered, overreact, or go into a fit of rage. It's also great to write about what is going through your mind when you get triggered in an honest and non-judgemental way. This practice can help you identify your patterns later and understand what triggers you the most.

Visualizing

People have been using several visualization exercises for centuries; however, they often get a bad rep for being too holistic. But the truth is that these techniques can be highly beneficial and are used by professional athletes to CEOs. Visualization is the technique of imagining your future as if it has already happened. This practice harnesses the power of the brain that cannot tell the difference between something that has already happened and something you imagine has happened.

With anxious attachment, visualization exercises can be used as a mental rehearsal, where you imagine yourself in a triggering situation and follow a set-out process to soothe yourself, calm your nervous system, and respond from a place of calm instead of fear. This exercise will help you mentally rehearse your reactions.

Mindfulness meditation helps you learn to stay with complicated feelings without analyzing, suppressing, or encouraging them. Allowing yourself to feel and acknowledge your worries, irritations, painful memories, and other emotions often helps them deplete. It provides a safe space to explore thoughts and feelings without judgment or shame. Try to ground yourself in the present moment for a simple exercise and listen to your breath. Bring the focus on the body and try noticing your bodily sensations without attaching meaning to them. If a thought comes up, notice it and let it pass. Stay there observing the body for as long as you can.

Positive affirmations are statements you repeat to yourself daily, grounding yourself in a new reality you create through them. They can be incredibly beneficial for anxiously attached people simply because they provide a way to shift negative thought patterns. Try connecting them with a calming breathing exercise, and repeat them when anxiety arises. Try writing them down in a notebook if you find it difficult to say them out loud or in your head. While beneficial, positive affirmations in themselves will not advance the healing process. You must do the groundwork of discovering and reframing your negative patterns, catching your negative self-talk, and reframing old, dysfunctional thought patterns before applying them successfully.

Belly breathing, also called diaphragmatic breathing, is a breathing technique you can hugely benefit from. Its positive impacts include reducing your blood pressure and heart rate and helping you relax more easily. When you breathe normally, you don't use your total lung capacity; however, with diaphragmatic breathing, you can help increase lung efficiency. It's proven to help you relax, increase the amount of oxygen in your blood, and reduce blood pressure and heart rate. It's believed to help reduce anxiety and normalize our body's response in stressful situations.

Picking up or touching items near you and paying attention to how they feel in your hands. Are they heavy or light, sharp or smooth? What is the color, the texture, the consistency, etc.? It is a fantastic exercise to instantly soothe yourself when emotionally overwhelmed, and you can practice it virtually anywhere.

My favorite mindfulness technique, however, is simply **noticing your surroundings**. Use all your senses to notice what's happening around you, no matter where you are. What can you see, smell, hear, taste, or touch? Make an effort to notice the little things you might not always pay attention to, like the color of the cars on the street or the noise your feet make when touching the ground.

THE CYCLE OF SELF-SOOTHING

I talked about visualizing exercises in an earlier chapter, and this is where it comes into play. Imagine a triggering situation and try to feel all the associated feelings: fear, anger, jealousy, etc. Now think of how you could respond to this situation from a calm and collected space. Imagine what you would do, what you would say, how you would react. Build a framework that suits you. This exercise will help you practice your reactions in anticipation of being triggered. It will solidify the self-soothing process, ensuring you reflect and respond instead of reacting in triggering situations.

A complete self-soothing cycle looks like this:

➤ I'm triggered by my partner's reaction and feel overwhelmed, but I pause before I habitually react.

➤ I take myself out of the triggering situation. I clear my head and return to my body by walking, shaking my arms, splashing cold water on my face, etc.

➤ Then I ask myself where the triggering feeling comes from. Is it based on reality? Is it connected to one of my core wounds?

➤ I acknowledge the feeling and fear behind the trigger and try to rewrite the thought I associate with it: "My partner's reaction doesn't reflect on me. They probably just had a bad day."

➤ I return to my partner when I'm calm and express my feelings. I ask them to clarify the problem, reassure me if needed, and work to resolve the issue if there is any. (Often, the trigger that comes up has nothing to do with our partner; instead, it's an unhealed core wound.)

➤ I accept the outcome and work to repair our connection or notice what parts of me need healing and make sure to do the work.

Rehearse the situation in your head as often as needed and practice staying calm. Rehearsing your reaction to the triggering event will help you build a solid self-soothing strategy that you can resort to when needed.

IMAGINE THAT YOU ARE IN A TRIGGERING SITUATION! HOW DO YOU CALM
YOURSELF AND PRACTICE SELF-SOOTHING?

_____

_____

_____

_____

_____

_____

_____

IMAGINE THAT YOUR PARTNER TRIGGERS YOU. WHAT DO YOU DO TO RESOLVE
THE PROBLEM AND COMMUNICATE YOUR NEEDS OR BOUNDARIES?

_____

_____

_____

_____

_____

_____

_____

WHAT ARE OUR CORE NEEDS?

There are core needs in our lives that form the basis of every choice, providing us with contentment and satisfaction. If these needs go unmet, the quality of our lives will likely diminish, and we will use compensating behaviors to make up for them in other areas of our lives. There are six core needs, of which the first four are personal. The need for certainty and variety are paradoxes, so if you experience an excess of one, you might find the other one lacking. The same applies to significance, and love and connection. For example, if you have an abundance of significance in your life – you're a high achiever, reaching all your career goals – you might find that your personal life or romantic life is lagging. The final two needs, growth, and significance are spiritual needs. They provide an essential foundation for fulfillment and happiness.

Need for certainty

This includes stability, consistency, security, control, safety, and predictability. With the need for certainty, we require a sense of stability in our lives. We need to know and understand that there are fixed elements in our lives that we can count on. We need to feel assured that we are safe, that we can avoid hurt, and that our lives and circumstances are predictable.

➤ Wanting to go to the same restaurant
➤ Wanting to keep our job in the long-term
➤ In for long-term partnerships and marriage

Need for variety

The opposite of certainty. It includes the need for variety, challenges, excitement, adventure, change, and novelty. The need for variety calls for change and adventure. It is the need for the unknown and new stimuli, whether it's a new job, a new home, getting to know new people, or going on a trip with our significant other.

➤ Liking adventure in our partnerships
➤ Taking a creative approach to our lives
➤ Celebrating the differences between the partners
➤ Spending time apart to recharge

Need for significance

This is the need to have meaning in our lives, a sense of importance, feeling needed, and wanted, and being worthy of love, etc. Significance is all about knowing that we are seen, that we matter, and that we're a priority to our partner. And it's about feeling it too. We experience significance in very different ways. Some of us need a quiet achievement, while others enjoy the spotlight. Either way, this core need centers around feeling unique, special, or needed.

➤ Needing to feel appreciated in our relationship
➤ Wanting our partner to voice or show how much they care for us

Need for love and connection

This is the need for communication, approval, attachment, feeling intimate, and being loved by other human beings. As humans, we need connection. The quality of our connections, friendships, or relationships hugely contributes to our mental and emotional health.

Need for growth

More of a spiritual need, it provides a structure for fulfillment and happiness; this is the need for constant spiritual, intellectual, and emotional growth, whether personal or romantic. All adult relationships go through stages of development, and it's crucial to follow along with understanding and compassion. For anxious attachers, accepting the passing of the honeymoon phase can be challenging, as it's our ideal state with heightened emotions and constant contact with our partner. But healthy relationship growth follows each new stage, and we must be open to accepting and appreciating them.

Need for contribution

Much like the previous one, this is also a spiritual need, the need to give, care, protect and provide beyond our own needs, the need to give back. By contributing, we hope to improve the lives of others and their physical, mental, or emotional state. If the interaction has made the other person feel better, even in a small way, you contributed to someone else's life.

WHAT DO YOU NEED TO FEEL SAFE IN A RELATIONSHIP?

Accountability	The ability to repair and reconnect after conflict
To be heard and seen by my partner	Healthy boundaries, and getting help in navigating them
To have my needs and boundaries respected	That my partner understands my attachment style and helps me heal
That my partner is open to work on themselves if needed	That my partner is able to handle conflict in a mature and healthy way
Clear and honest communication	Transparency and integrity
That my partner chooses to work on the relationship with me	That I can count on my partner in difficult situations

WHAT ARE THE KEY THINGS YOU NEED MORE OF FROM YOUR PARTNER OR FUTURE PARTNER? HOW COULD YOU COMMUNICATE THIS TO THEM?

_____

_____

_____

_____

_____

_____

_____

WHAT DOES LOVE MEAN TO YOU IN A PRACTICAL, EVERYDAY SENSE? WHAT ARE THE SMALL DAILY ACTIONS THAT MAKE YOU FEEL LOVED?

_____

_____

_____

_____

_____

_____

_____

WHAT DOES A FULFILLING RELATIONSHIP MEAN TO YOU? WHAT ARE YOUR NON-NEGOTIABLES IN A PARTNERSHIP?

_____

_____

_____

_____

_____

_____

_____

WHAT COULD YOU BE MORE FLEXIBLE ABOUT? WHAT ARE THE ANXIOUSLY WIRED NEEDS THAT YOU COULD RELAX A LITTLE OR MEET YOURSELF?

_____

_____

_____

_____

_____

_____

_____

DO YOU HAVE RIGID EXPECTATIONS FOR SPECIFIC OUTCOMES? DO YOU FEEL
DISAPPOINTED, OR LET DOWN WHEN THESE EXPECTATIONS AREN'T MET?

_____

_____

_____

_____

_____

_____

_____

HOW COULD YOU OFFER YOURSELF A DIFFERENT PERSPECTIVE ON THESE
OUTCOMES? HOW COULD YOU SHOW A LITTLE MORE FLEXIBILITY IN THE
RELATIONSHIP?

_____

_____

_____

_____

_____

_____

REACTING VS RESPONDING

As anxious attachers, we tend to react harshly and impulsively to situations that make us uncomfortable. A reaction is unconscious and is often an instant consequence of a trigger. It is created based on our internalized beliefs and biases. When we say or do something without thinking it through, that's our unconscious mind running the show.

A reaction is based on the moment and doesn't consider the long-term consequences of what we do or say. A reaction is survival-oriented and, on some level, a defense mechanism. When we react, it's often out of fear. It shows a lack of self-reflection and is motivated by wanting a need met, getting more attention, or closeness. Reacting looks like sudden outbursts of anger: raising our voices, slamming doors, deflecting instead of taking responsibility.

A response usually comes more slowly and is based on information from the conscious and subconscious mind. **A response takes into consideration the well-being of not only you but those around you. Responding means reflection and consideration.** It considers the long-term consequences of our immediate actions and is influenced by our prefrontal cortex, the logical thinking part of the brain. Responding shows awareness and consideration. It is driven by a need to repair, get closer, and deepen the relationship. There is an intentional choice behind responding, the choice of being authentic and open about our emotions, flaws, and triggers.

Think of your triggers and trauma reactions and determine which has the most profound impact on your current relationship. Try to be objective when you do this exercise. Shaming or blaming yourself is not going to help the process.

The practice is simple. Take one of your anxiously attached patterns, and think about how to turn it around to benefit your relationship.

Here is an example of the exercise:

The triggering situation: "My partner checks out other people."

My old pattern: "This triggers a deep-rooted anxiety and the core wound of feeling worthless, and I respond by shutting down and giving them the silent treatment."

I will change my reaction by: "Finding ways to boost my self-esteem. I will also take a deep breath when this happens again and let my partner know – in a calm and collected manner – how this behavior makes me feel."

The thought I rewrite in my head: "I'm learning to value my worth by building my self-esteem. I know that my partner loves me and that looking at other people does not impact my worth or my partner's love for me."

The change impacts my life and relationships: "I feel more confident now that I have become more secure in my values. Bringing up the problem to my partner made me realize that my needs and boundaries will not push them away, which feels reassuring."

Practice rewiring your reactions

Focus on exchanging the response to the trigger by associating it with the unbiased truth or a positive thought pattern. Swapping your intrusive thoughts or perceived feelings of a threat to the reality of the situation will help you calm down and leave a positive impact in the long run. The more you practice this, the easier it will be to tap into it every time you get triggered.

Intrusive thought	Conscious reflection
My partner wants to spend the weekend alone, making me anxious and fearful, as I believe they no longer love me.	Taking time out of a relationship can be healthy for both of us, and my partner's need for alone time doesn't reflect on me. I will use this time to catch up with my friends and reconnect with myself.
I get anxious whenever I catch my partner checking their phone and smiling. My first reaction is that they are having an affair.	Having close friendships or a great social life outside the relationship is healthy. I believe my partner loves me, is faithful to me, and I don't have any reason to doubt him or our relationship.

Intrusive thought	Conscious reflection

DO YOU HAVE RIGID EXPECTATIONS FOR SPECIFIC OUTCOMES? DO YOU FEEL
DISAPPOINTED, OR LET DOWN WHEN THESE EXPECTATIONS AREN'T MET?

_____

_____

_____

_____

_____

_____

_____

HOW COULD YOU OFFER YOURSELF A DIFFERENT PERSPECTIVE ON THESE
OUTCOMES? HOW COULD YOU SHOW A LITTLE MORE FLEXIBILITY IN THE
RELATIONSHIP?

_____

_____

_____

_____

_____

_____

DO YOU HAVE A SITUATION OR BEHAVIOUR THAT YOU ALWAYS OVERREACT TO?

_____

_____

_____

_____

_____

_____

_____

HOW COULD YOU SHARE THIS WITH YOUR PARTNER COMING FROM A PLACE OF REFLECTION INSTEAD OF REACTING IN THE MOMENT?

_____

_____

_____

_____

_____

_____

_____

CO-REGULATION VS CO-DEPENDENCY IN RELATIONSHIPS

Co-regulation in relationships is when the partners help each other to regulate their emotions and reduce stress effectively. Co-regulation can happen through physical touch, holding hands, hugging, speaking soothingly, or verbal acknowledgment of distress. To effectively co-regulate with your partner, learn each other's preferred way of being heard, seen, and reassured. Often we want to be validated rather than offered a solution, so get into the habit of asking one another if you need active listening or a solution to your problem. Remember, co-regulation is a choice and cannot be forced or demanded.

Active listening. Stay present with your partner when they share something with you, even if it's painful to hear. Shift the focus from defending yourself or explaining your behavior to empathizing with your partner's feelings. Put yourself in their shoes and stay present. What we often need beyond a viable solution is someone who can hear, see, and empathise with us. So being an active listener for your partner can go a long way.

Empathizing means putting yourself in your partner's shoes working towards understanding their feelings and pain, and validating it while holding space for your own. Being able to read your partner's body language effectively will help a lot, as often we express anger while we have underlying feelings of sadness or loneliness. With anxious attachment, our first instinct when facing a problem might be to try and solve or fix it. So instead, try to stay present with your partner and show them compassion. This 'shared pain' will help you connect on a deeper level.

Co-dependency happens when the partners are reliant on each other emotionally, mentally, or physically. Co-dependency is very likely developed around our attachment patterns and is very common with anxious attachment. It involves putting our partners on a pedestal, walking on eggshells around them, and regularly trying to rescue our partners, fix them, or save them. With codependency, we struggle to find time for ourselves, or put our needs and wants first. As it develops, it gives us a strong feeling of being lost in our relationship, and becoming one with our partner's lives. It can be really challenging to remove ourselves from a co-dependent dynamic, as we might feel that our partner relies on us, or that we are the only source of help, safety, or comfort for our partner. However, with self-awareness, we can start to recognize our patterns, take steps to set boundaries, and shift the focus back on ourselves.

DO YOU FEEL YOU HAVE A CO-DEPENDENT DYNAMIC IN YOUR RELATIONSHIP?

_____

_____

_____

_____

_____

_____

WHAT COULD YOU DO TO SHIFT THE FOCUS BACK ON YOURSELF, WHILE
STILL SHOWING LOVE AND APPRECIATION TO YOUR PARTNER?

_____

_____

_____

_____

_____

_____

DO YOU EVER OVERSTEP YOUR PARTNER'S BOUNDARIES TRYING TO FIX, SAVE THEM, OR TAKE CARE OF THEM?

_____

_____

_____

_____

_____

_____

_____

WHAT WOULD YOU LIKE TO CHANGE IN YOURSELF TO DEVELOP A MORE INTERDEPENDENT RELATIONSHIP?

_____

_____

_____

_____

_____

_____

_____

HOW TO SET BOUNDARIES?

A boundary is a healthy guideline we create to protect ourselves, our well-being, and our autonomy. Boundaries can help us retain a sense of identity and personal space, and they're easier to create and maintain than one might think. Setting boundaries means asking our partner to meet our needs and respecting our choices in life and the relationship.

Establishing and maintaining boundaries as anxiously attached can be difficult, for we are predisposed to believe that people will not respect them. So we either don't set any or hold onto inflexible ones. Personal boundaries are important to set and respect; however, if we grow up thinking that we need to bend and adjust our ways to please others, it can be pretty challenging to learn them as adults.

Setting boundaries is simply about communicating your needs to someone else. It isn't always easy. Not everyone will understand your needs because not everyone shares these needs. So let's review a few anxiously attached needs and how to set boundaries around them.

You need frequent reassurance from your partner:
➤ " I know you love me, but I would appreciate it if you could find a way to express it more often."

You cannot handle uncertainty in the relationship:
➤ "I would like us to talk about where we are in the relationship and where we're heading. I'm picking up on mixed signals and find them confusing."

You have bouts of anxiety every time your partner asks for time alone:
➤ "I understand that you need time for yourself, and I completely respect this. But could you check in so I know I'm important to you?"

You need your partner to discuss problems instead of shutting down:
➤ "I understand that it is difficult for you to talk about relationship problems, but let's try and find a way to resolve our issues. Let me know what you feel most comfortable with, and we'll work something out."

WHAT ARE THE MOST IMPORTANT BOUNDARIES THAT YOU NEED TO FEEL SAFE AND RESPECTED IN YOUR RELATIONSHIP?

_____

_____

_____

_____

_____

_____

_____

WHAT SELF-BOUNDARIES CAN YOU SET TO IMPROVE YOUR LIFE AND RELATIONAL DYNAMIC?

_____

_____

_____

_____

_____

_____

_____

IMAGINE BEING LET DOWN BY YOUR PARTNER. NOW TRY TO COUNTERACT THE FEELING BY LISTING OUT ALL THE WAYS YOUR PARTNER SHOWS YOU LOVE AND AFFECTION AND SUPPORTS YOU.

_____

_____

_____

_____

_____

_____

CAN YOU RECALL A SITUATION WHERE YOU FELT YOUR PARTNER LET YOU DOWN? TRY TO REEVALUATE YOUR FEELINGS. IS THERE ANY WIGGLE ROOM FOR YOUR PARTNER'S WAY OR PERSPECTIVE?

_____

_____

_____

_____

_____

_____

TRY TO RECALL A TRIGGERING SITUATION; FIGHT OR CONFLICT FROM YOUR RELATIONSHIP. NOW PUT YOURSELF IN YOUR PARTNER'S SHOES. CAN YOU EMPATHISE WITH THEM? CAN YOU AGREE WITH THEIR VERSION OF TRUTH?

_____

_____

_____

_____

_____

_____

WHAT DOES EMOTIONAL VALIDATION MEAN TO YOU? HOW DO YOU WANT TO RECEIVE IT AND HOW CAN YOU VALIDATE YOUR PARTNER?

_____

_____

_____

_____

_____

_____

_____

WHAT DOES EMOTIONAL SELF-VALIDATION SOUND LIKE?

My needs matter too, so I can make myself a priority.

It's okay to be upset over this, my feelings are valid no matter what others think.

My thoughts and feelings are important even if my partner can't validate them.

I am not perfect, but I'm making progress every day.

It's okay to reassure myself and not wait for external validation all the time.

Wanting an explanation or clarity about my relationship doesn't make needy.

Even though I'm anxiously attached, the problem is not always me.

I am the best judge of what is good for me and what isn't.

I will make time to celebrate my own success because I deserve it.

I don't need to prove my worth to anyone.

I prioritize my mental health, so I step away from this argument.

I don't have to work hard to earn love, I deserve to be loved for who I am.

HOW COULD YOU VALIDATE YOUR OWN EMOTIONS IN TRIGGERING
SITUATIONS? HOW CAN YOU HOLD SPACE FOR YOUR FEELINGS AS WELL AS
YOUR PARTNER'S NEEDS?

_____

_____

_____

_____

_____

_____

_____

WHAT IS THE MOST COMMON PATTERN THAT KEEPS RESURFACING IN YOUR
RELATIONSHIP? WHY DO YOU THINK IT KEEPS COMING UP?

_____

_____

_____

_____

_____

_____

_____

TRIGGERS AND OUR EMOTIONAL RESPONSES

Our feelings aren't just reactions. They are our brain's way of making sense of the information and physical sensations around us. When we realize this, we can start using emotions to understand ourselves better. **We benefit in many ways by developing the ability to understand and express our emotions. We can manage stress better, communicate with others, and develop self-compassion.** We should not suppress our feelings; instead, we should use them as pointers to discover our core needs and values.

Emotional literacy takes us one step closer to understanding ourselves. It also makes it easier to express our feelings to our partners. The primary benefit, however, is understanding that emotions have a way of triggering survival behaviors in us. **Human emotions have developed through evolution as a survival mechanism, and when we understand what they're trying to signal, we can address the real need under the surface.** If we don't, we keep reliving our negative stories attached to the core beliefs we formed as children. This results in repeating the same relational patterns, feeling the same feelings, and thinking the same thoughts without questioning their validity.

An example of unconscious pattern repetition:

➤ A triggering event happens to us. This triggers an internalized issue: unresolved past patterns, insecurities, fear, anxiety, core wounds, etc.
➤ As a response, we unconsciously create a story around this event and make assumptions as to why this is happening
➤ These assumptions now influence our reactions, feelings, and thoughts
➤ We act out on these thoughts and unconsciously reinforce them through our negative thought patterns
➤ The core belief is now reinforced proving to us the negative meaning we attached to the original story

This happens because our brain has a way of protecting us by creating negative stories and attaching negative meanings to events. The brain considers uncertainty dangerous, so a negative story feels like a 'much safer choice'. This practice of creating self-fulfilling prophecies prevents us from getting hurt or exposing ourselves to further danger.

TRY TO DESCRIBE THE EMOTIONS THAT COME UP WHEN YOU'RE TRIGGERED. THIS HELPS CREATE SPACE BETWEEN YOU AND THE NEGATIVE EVENT, HELPING YOU ENGAGE IN REFLECTION, RATHER THAN REACTING.

_____

_____

_____

_____

_____

_____

WHAT ARE THE MOST COMMON NEGATIVE EMOTIONS THAT COME UP IN YOUR RELATIONSHIPS? CAN YOU WORK OUT WHERE THESE FEELINGS COME FROM? ARE THEY CONNECTED TO YOUR CURRENT RELATIONSHIP, OR PERHAPS A PAST TRAUMA, SITUATION, PAIN, ETC.?

_____

_____

_____

_____

_____

_____

WHAT IS THE MOST COMMON FEELING THAT COMES UP WHEN YOU'RE TRIGGERED? CAN YOU IDENTIFY IT? CAN YOU CONNECT IT TO AN AGE OR TIME IN YOUR LIFE?

_____

_____

_____

_____

_____

_____

WHAT DOES THIS VERSION OF YOU NEED TO FEEL SAFE? ARE YOU PERHAPS 6 YEARS OLD AND NEED VALIDATION FROM YOUR MOM? ARE YOU IN YOUR LATE 20S AND NEED EMOTIONAL STABILITY IN YOUR LIFE?

_____

_____

_____

_____

_____

HOW CAN YOU MEET THIS NEED? WHAT CAN YOU GIVE TO THIS VERSION OF YOURSELF TO FEEL SAFE, REASSURED, AND VALIDATED?

_____

_____

_____

_____

_____

_____

WHAT CALMS YOU DOWN THE MOST IN A DIFFICULT OR TRIGGERING SITUATION?

_____

_____

_____

_____

_____

_____

_____

THE PRACTICE OF SELF-REPARENTING

By reparenting yourself, you can tune into all the love, respect, and care you craved but perhaps never received as a child. This process will allow you to feel stable, happy, and balanced. You will become less sensitive to triggers and less likely to seek external validation. Here are some of my reparenting best practices:

Rewrite your negative self-talk

Spot your negative self-talk, and replace it with a positive one. Rewiring negative self-talk can happen in many ways, but the quickest and most effective is teaching your brain that the opposite of the negative belief is true. To achieve this you need to train yourself to find instances when the opposite of the negative thought or your core belief happens, no matter how big or small. Then work to bring your attention to it, internalize it, and feel it. For example, you keep telling yourself that you are unworthy, so you look to find instances when the opposite is proven, for example, someone gives up their seat for you on a train or holds the door open for you at the store.

Get in touch with your real needs and meet them

This is a powerful next step in the reparenting process. Learn to ask yourself your real needs daily and work to meet them. It might be overwhelming or confusing initially because you are likely wired to neglect your needs to maintain a connection with your attachment figure. But don't get discouraged. Just keep going until it becomes natural.

Celebrate the small wins

Keep noticing the small wins. Establish a routine where you accomplish something small every day. No matter what it is, no matter if it doesn't make sense to anyone else. This will work as a positive reinforcement making it easier to achieve anything the next time.

And most importantly, do not overwhelm yourself. It takes time and daily investment to establish safety in your body, so go slow and recognize the change on your way. Instead of focusing on the big win, notice and celebrate the person you are becoming.

SPOT YOUR NEGATIVE SELF-TALK. WRITE DOWN EVERY NEGATIVE THOUGHT AND INNER CHATTER YOU KEEP REPEATING!

_____

_____

_____

_____

_____

_____

HOW COULD YOU REPLACE THESE WITH POSITIVE, SELF-ASSURING LANGUAGE? TRY TO FIND INSTANCES THAT MAKE YOU FEEL WORTHY!

_____

_____

_____

_____

_____

_____

_____

WRITE DOWN EVERY ACHIEVEMENT, BIG OR SMALL YOU REACHED THIS WEEK, MONTH, OR YEAR! EVEN THE SMALL ONES.

_____

_____

_____

_____

_____

_____

HOW COULD YOU REWARD YOURSELF? HOW COULD YOU CELEBRATE THESE ACHIEVEMENTS, EVEN IN A SMALL WAY?

_____

_____

_____

_____

_____

_____

_____

LETTING GO OF PAST HURT AND PRACTICING FORGIVENESS

I would like to preface this chapter by saying that forgiveness is optional. **You don't have to forgive or forget to move on and find peace, but letting go of past hurts will help you immensely in the healing process.** While it might be tempting to hold a grudge against someone, and it might even feel like we are holding them accountable, in most cases, it's not worth our emotional health or inner peace.

If you decide to forgive someone, it doesn't minimize the impact of their actions on your life. However, it might bring you peace and possibly even relief from the negative emotions and thoughts you hold on to. This might help you reach the much-needed release from all the anxious thoughts, ruminating and replaying past situations or conversations in your head over and over.

With anxious attachment, it is pretty common to experience an 'external forgiveness.' This type of forgiveness is spoken or expressed outwards only, and it doesn't reflect a sense of relief from negative emotions, such as anger and hurt. So we often hold onto past hurts, even long after the breakup or a conflict. **Releasing these negative emotions through forgiveness might help us speed up the healing process and find a better footing in our relationship without holding onto grudges or expecting our current or future partner to make up for past mistakes.**

Letting go of past hurts makes you much stronger, more resilient, and one step closer to securely attaching in your next relationship. Releasing your emotional baggage will help you focus on the way forward and give you space to deal with your healing rather than constantly thinking about what if and why. This will prevent accumulating more emotional baggage that we carry with us and refocus our attention on ourselves.

DO YOU HAVE A PAST SITUATION THAT LEFT YOU FEELING DEPLETED, OR BROKEN? CAN YOU PRACTICE FORGIVING YOURSELF OR YOUR PARTNER FOR THIS SITUATION?

_____

_____

_____

_____

_____

_____

_____

HOW COULD YOU PRACTICE FORGIVING YOURSELF FOR YOUR PAST MISTAKES OR FAULTS?

_____

_____

_____

_____

_____

_____

_____

IMAGINE THAT YOUR NEEDS AND FEELINGS ARE NOT MET BY YOUR PARTNER. HOW COULD YOU SOOTHE YOURSELF AND REFLECT ON THIS FROM A SECURE PLACE?

_____

_____

_____

_____

_____

TELL ME A PAST SITUATION THAT YOU BLAME YOURSELF FOR. HOW WOULD YOU RESOLVE THIS SITUATION TODAY? WHAT WOULD YOU DO DIFFERENTLY?

_____

_____

_____

_____

_____

_____

TELL ME ABOUT YOUR MOST PAINFUL BREAKUP! WHAT DID YOU LEARN
ABOUT YOURSELF? WHAT WAS YOUR KEY TAKEAWAY?

_____

_____

_____

_____

_____

_____

WHAT IS YOUR BIGGEST RELATIONSHIP REGRET OR MISTAKE? WHAT WOULD
YOU DO DIFFERENTLY TODAY AND WHY?

_____

_____

_____

_____

_____

_____

WHAT IS YOUR BIGGEST FEAR IN A RELATIONSHIP AND WHY?

_____

_____

_____

_____

_____

_____

_____

WHAT EMOTIONS AND INSECURITIES ARE BEHIND THIS FEAR? CAN YOU CONNECT THIS TO A CORE WOUND OR A PAST HURT?

_____

_____

_____

_____

_____

_____

_____

TRY TO QUESTION THESE INSECURE THOUGHTS! DO THEY REFLECT ON YOUR CURRENT SITUATION? HAVE YOU ALWAYS HAD THEM?

_____

_____

_____

_____

_____

_____

IF THEY ARE RECURRING PATTERNS, WHERE DO THEY COME FROM? WHEN WAS THE FIRST TIME YOU THOUGHT/FELT THEM?

_____

_____

_____

_____

_____

_____

PRACTICE REWRITING YOUR INSECURITIES WITH A SIMPLE EXERCISE! WRITE DOWN ALL OF THEM, THEN WRITE DOWN AN EXAMPLE THAT PROVES THE OPPOSITE!

I am not good enough, and I'm always overlooked.	**Yesterday I got a really nice compliment from a complete stranger at the gym.**
I don't deserve great things in life.	**Last January I was promoted at my job with a pay rise. I deserve great things!**

CULTIVATING SECURE BEST PRACTICES IN YOUR RELATIONSHIP

Even if you didn't have an upbringing that helped you develop a secure attachment style, it is totally possible to cultivate an earned secure attachment as an adult. It starts with emotional awareness and developing the ability to feel safe even when alone.

Here are some key steps:

Learn to identify and express your emotions to yourself and others calmly—no blaming, shaming, pointing the finger, projecting, or stonewalling. Identifying and connecting our feelings with our core needs will be crucial in the learning process. If you recognize the emotion and the need behind it, you create a chance to solve a problem, state a need, or create a boundary. You can then effectively communicate it to your partner and work together to meet each other's needs.

Aim for integrity and look for partners who exhibit it. Securely attached people exhibit behaviors that align with who they say they are and what they say they will do.

Talk about real stuff, and share your relationship concerns with your partner. Be upfront and be brave. Being securely attached doesn't mean you are entirely free of worries, but securely attached folks can easily share their concerns with their partner. This looks like pointing out potential or future problems, sharing your triggers and anxiously attached behavior, and showing up as your most authentic self in the partnership.

Work to discover your patterns, and triggers and recognize when your anxious attachment runs the show, and share this with your partner. Let them know what happens when you feel threatened, when you get triggered, and how you act when your attachment system gets activated. Sharing your attachment issues and opening up vulnerably will help your partner understand your anxious attachment activation and give them a cue to co-regulate with you and solve the problem together.

Purge toxic relationships and behavior from your life. Work to reduce the times you are subjected to anything that triggers or sends your nervous system into fight or flight mode. The easiest way to achieve this is to date securely attached people, however, this isn't always possible.

So work to reduce the times you get triggered by recognizing what triggers you and laying clear and firm boundaries around this behavior, whether with your partner or yourself. Pay attention to your reactions in triggering situations and learn to recognize them when they happen so that you can leave and self-regulate. Work to limit your time around people or situations that trigger you.

Learn the fine line between leaning on someone for support or validation and being co-dependent on them. There is a massive difference between healthy co-regulation and codependency. Healthy co-regulation considers the partner's mood and availability and involves consent. Co-dependency is self-centered. It only focuses on the self, leading with neediness and demands. We have to recognize that our partner isn't there to reassure and validate us, so we need to learn to shoulder some of the responsibility by creating a healthy support system of family and friends and by learning healthy self-regulation and self-validation.

Get curious about your partner. Ask them questions, get to know who they are, and how they make decisions. Learn about their childhood, their past traumas, previous relationships, how they like to relax, and how they solve problems. Don't assume what your partner feels or thinks if there is a problem, miscommunication, or misunderstanding. Ask them to clarify. Talk about needs and boundaries, and work to understand your partner's perspective and thinking. We all come from very different family backgrounds, have different upbringings, and see the world entirely differently. We need to share our versions with each other to avoid conflicts.

Work to understand how you contribute to your relationship dynamics. This applies to both partners. Understanding how and why our behavior impacts our relationship will help us change it and establish mutual ground regarding conflict resolution. Focus on the most common recurring patterns and work to solve or eliminate them first. What is the source of most of your problems? What do you have constant arguments around? Is it spending time together or apart, involving friends in the partnership, communicating (or not) wants and needs, setting boundaries around your resources, or perhaps the availability of your partner? Knowing your part of the equation helps set things right and work through conflict easier, not to mention it can help prevent recurring problems.

"THE BEST RELATIONSHIPS AREN'T BUILT ON PARTNERS MOSTLY TELLING EACH OTHER WHAT'S WRONG.

THEY'RE BUILT ON PARTNERS MOSTLY TELLING EACH OTHER WHAT'S RIGHT"

BRENE BROWN

IMAGINE YOURSELF AS YOUR MOST SECURE SELF. WRITE DOWN ALL THE GREAT QUALITIES, THOUGHT PATTERNS, AND NEW WAYS YOU HAVE. HOW WILL YOU GET THERE FROM WHERE YOU ARE NOW?

_____

_____

_____

_____

_____

_____

HOW CAN YOU PRACTICE VALIDATING YOUR THOUGHTS AND FEELINGS, AND BUILD AN INTERDEPENDENT RELATIONSHIP WITH YOUR PARTNER?

_____

_____

_____

_____

_____

_____

_____

HOW CAN YOU REWARD YOURSELF DURING THE HEALING JOURNEY? WHAT WILL KEEP YOU MOTIVATED EVEN WHEN YOUR PROGRESS IS SLOWER THAN EXPECTED?

_____

_____

_____

_____

_____

_____

HOW WILL YOU START SHIFTING TOWARDS SECURE BEST PRACTICES? WHAT WILL YOU PRIORITISE, AND WHAT DO YOU WANT TO CHANGE?

_____

_____

_____

_____

_____

_____

WHAT IS YOUR KEY TAKEAWAY FROM THE JOURNAL?

ALMOST EVERYTHING GREAT BEGINS WITH A TERRIBLE FIRST EFFORT. GETTING STARTED CHANGES EVERYTHING.

Thank you for being here, opening up, and getting curious about your most painful memories and biggest fears. Trust me when I say you are already a massive step closer to creating a secure attachment in your relationship. Remember that healing comes with consistency, effort, and self-acceptance.

Keep practicing the exercises you learned in the workbook to continue your healing journey. Keep pausing and reflecting. Practice honest and open communication, setting boundaries, and honoring yourself without fear of judgment from others. But most importantly, love yourself the way you want others to love you.

ROMI

REFERENCES

Bowlby, John (1988). A Secure Base: Parent-Child Attachment and Healthy Human Development

Bryans, Janis PSY.D (2021) Anxious Attachment, Coping Strategies To Deal With Anxiety, Insecurity, Fear Of Abandonment And Reconnect With Your Partner

Chan, Annie LMFT (2019). The Attachment Theory Workbook: Powerful Tools to Promote Understanding, Increase Stability, and Build Lasting Relationships

Lawson, David Ph.D. (2020). Insecure Attachment: Anxious or Avoidant in Love? How attachment styles help or hurt your relationships. Learn to form secure emotional connections

LePera, Nicole (2021). How To Do The Work: Recognize Your Patterns, Heal from Your Past, and Create Your Self

Levine, Amir (2012). Attached. The New Science of Adult Attachment and How It Can Help You Find - and Keep - Love

Siegel, Romi (2023) The Anxious Attachment Handbook, A Practical Guide to Heal Your Anxious Attachment and Improve Your Relationship